New Hymns for the Life of the Church

NEW HYMNS
FOR THE LIFE OF THE CHURCH

To Make Our Prayer and Music One

Music by Carol Doran
Words by Thomas H. Troeger

New York   Oxford
OXFORD UNIVERSITY PRESS
1992

Oxford University Press

Oxford   New York   Toronto
Delhi   Bombay   Calcutta   Madras   Karachi
Kuala Lumpur   Singapore   Hong Kong   Tokyo
Nairobi   Dar es Salaam   Cape Town
Melbourne   Auckland   Madrid

and associated companies in
Berlin   Ibadan

Copyright © 1992 by Oxford University Press, Inc.

Published by Oxford University Press, Inc.
200 Madison Avenue, New York, New York 10016

Oxford is a registered trademark of Oxford University Press, Inc.

Permissions note:
Prompt arrangements can be made for permission for a church congregation
to reproduce single hymns for service use,
as well as for the wider use of the copyrighted material in this book.
In North and South America, apply to Oxford University Press, New York, Music Department.
Elsewhere in the world, apply to Oxford, England.
Hymn Copyright Department.

Library of Congress Cataloging-in-Publication Data
Doran, Carol.
New hymns for the life of the church :
to make our prayer and music one /
music by Carol Doran : words by Thomas H. Troeger.
1 Score.   Includes index.   ISBN 0-19-385865-7
1. Hymns, English.
I. Troeger, Thomas H., 1945- .
II. Title.   M2117.D64N53   1992   92-11541   M

2 4 6 8 9 7 5 3 1

Printed in the United States of America
on acid free paper

Contents

Introduction, **vii**
The Hymns, **1**

I LIFE CYCLE NEEDS

the care of children

1. Our Savior's Infant Cries Were Heard, **2**

baptism, confirmation, reaffirmation of faith

2. If all You Want, Lord, Is My Heart, **4**
3. What King Would Wade Through Murky Streams, **6**

education

4. Praise the Source of Faith and Learning, **8**

marriage

5. We Need Each Other's Voice to Sing, **10**

dying

6. Risen Christ, May Death be Swift, **12**

grief

7. How Long, O Lord, How Long?, **14**

II SPECIAL CONGREGATIONAL NEEDS

celebrating ministries of music

8. Glory to God Is the Song of the Stars, **19**
9. Make Your Prayer and Music One, **22**

celebrating ministries of the word

10. The Rocks Would Shout if We Kept Still, **24**

confession and renewal

11. The Cross on the Hill Is the Measuring Rod, **26**

spiritual discipline

12. Eagles' Spiralings Comply, **28**
13. Let all Who Pray the Prayer Christ Taught, **30**
14. Through Our Fragmentary Prayers, **32**

ordination, commissioning, installation, consecration

15. Pastor, Lead Our Circle Dance, **34**

church anniversaries and rededications

16. We Travel Toward a Land Unknown, **36**
17. View the Present through the Promise, **38**

III THEOLOGICAL AND SOCIAL NEEDS

victims of abuse

18. Holy and Good Is the Gift of Desire, **43**

different kinds of families

19. God Made from One Blood all the Families of Earth, **46**

inclusive images for God

20. Source and Sovereign, Rock and Cloud, **48**

the search for faith

21. Ask, Seek, Knock, **50**
22. When There Is No Star to Guide You, **52**

the search for justice

23. The Least in God's Kingdom Is Greater than John, **54**

the search for peace

24. Fierce the Force that Curled Cain's Fist, **56**
25. Lions and Oxen Will Feed in the Hay, **58**

Notes, **61**
Metrical Index, **65**
Scriptural Index, **67**
Index by Pastoral Need, Special Occasion, and Liturgical Season, **69**
Index of First Lines, **73**
Index of Alternate Tunes, **75**

Introduction

HISTORICAL PRECEDENTS

Hymns have always reflected the character and concerns of the age that produced them. The psalmists reworked imagery common to the ancient Near East in order to express what they believed about YAHWEH. Paul the apostle quoted from a hymn that drew upon the cosmology of its day to express the love of Christ. John filled his apocalyptic vision with triumphant hymns to give hope to believers who suffered under the oppression of the Roman empire.

The process we trace in Scripture continued through the life of the church. Ambrose, bishop of Milan, wrote hymns to strengthen orthodox belief during a period of theological conflict. Through hymns, Luther carried his insights to the people and the Wesleys vitalized their movement. The hymns of African Americans helped them endure slavery and reach toward freedom. The leaders of the social gospel encouraged the church to work for justice through hymns.

The history of hymns reveals that faith is always seeking contemporary expression in worship. Obeying the psalmist's command, "Sing to the Lord a new song," the church makes clear that God is involved in the struggles of the human community. Through the creation of new hymns the church extends its pastoral care and prophetic witness by recognizing that the concerns of the people are worthy of being lifted up in songful worship.

CONTINUING THE TRADITION TODAY

We are attempting to continue this dynamic tradition by writing hymns that give voice to many of the theological, pastoral, and social concerns that mark our own age. These include greater attention to the transitions that accompany the life cycle, the abuse of women, the neglect of children, the inequalities of social and economic systems, the relationship of faith and learning, an appreciation for the variety of forms that families take, the search for peace, the care of the terminally ill, increasing liturgical concern for music and the other arts, finding language that is gracefully inclusive of women and men, and expressing divine reality through images that renew our sense of the holiness and mystery of God.

We have no illusion that it is easy for all people to sing about all of these matters. Through our daily work in ecumenical theological schools, and our leadership of workshops on worship renewal in Canada and the United States, we are familiar with the resistance to what is new:

> Far easier to melt the gold
>> And smash the brittle clay
> Of idols that the hand may mold
>> Than change the way we pray.
>
> How tempting for the church to seize
>> Upon familiar forms,
> Retreating to antiquities
>> To hide from present storms.   (THT)

But we are also familiar with the profound satisfaction that worshippers know when the church is bold enough to include in its hymns the vital concerns of our common life. We recall, for instance, a woman who acknowledged how moved she was by singing these lines from our hymn about various kinds of families:

> We turn to you, God, with our thanks and our tears
> For all of the families we've known through the years,
> The intimate networks on whom we depend
> Of parent and partner and roommate and friend.

Middle-aged and only recently married for the first time, she found herself filled with thanks for all those people who made up "the intimate networks" that had been her family for so many years.

It sounds a small thing in the telling of it, but such a moment can be an epiphany, a time when the truth and the meaning of people's lives become manifest. A flood of wonder breaks loose in their hearts, and their faith in God is strengthened in ways they had never imagined.

All of this happens not through words alone but through words sustained and lifted by music that stirs the visionary power in worshippers. We recall a service that concluded with another hymn from this book, "We Need Each Other's Voice to Sing." On the final time through the refrain, the sopranos supplied the descant as all sang together:

> We give our alleluias
>> to the church's common chord;
>> Alleluia! Alleluia!
> Praise, O praise, O praise the Lord!

Afterwards, a member of the congregation said, "When the sopranos came in and we sang the final note, I did not want it to end. For a moment we arrived where I am always hoping worship will lead us."

LEADERSHIP FROM CLERGY AND MUSICIANS

We tell these stories because they represent what is possible when worship leaders are willing to try new words and music. Of course, none of this automatically happens. The effectiveness of new hymns, like the other elements of the liturgy, depends upon the way they are presented and upon the working of the Spirit. Although the Spirit is not ours to control, those who lead the worshipping assembly, especially the clergy and pastoral musicians, have primary roles in effectively introducing new hymns.

Clergy and musicians need to consult one another to be certain that the hymn is appropriate for the occasion. When a hymn draws together the theme of the preaching or focuses the prayers of the people or serves in some other way to reinforce the theological integrity of the liturgy, then the congregation is much more receptive to its use. Instead of seeing the hymn as simply "one more new song," people experience it as an act of prayer.

It is also vital that the clergy, or whoever is presiding at the service, be visibly present before the congregation when the pastoral musician teaches the hymn prior to the service. We cannot overemphasize the importance of this. Groups do what leaders do, and if the leader models an earnest effort to follow the musician and to learn the new hymn, then the congregation will join in more enthusiastically.

Likewise, when the hymn is sung during the service, the liturgical leaders should wholeheartedly participate to show that the hymn is a vital part of the worship. If the leaders are otherwise occupied, they announce in effect to everyone else: it does not matter whether you sing this new hymn or not because it is simply filler music until the real action resumes.

ARRANGEMENT OF THE HYMNS

For each hymn, the text and the tune have been placed on the lefthand page facing the accompaniment on the right.* This arrangement allows the singers a clear presentation of the hymn without the distraction of the accompaniment, which only the accompanying musician needs. In addition, we hope that those who have requested permission to make copies of hymns for congregational use will find this new format more convenient and economical to reproduce.

HOW TO INTRODUCE NEW HYMN SETTINGS
TO THE CONGREGATION

The musician introducing the new hymn settings in this book will discover that they are accessible to congregations if the music is properly presented. The unison tunes

*The only exceptions are numbers 8 and 18, in which the accompaniment requires both facing pages. In these cases, the text and tune are printed on the preceding page. Permission is hereby given to make a single photocopy of the singers' version of each of these two hymns in order to arrange it on the music rack in the accompanist's sight.

are easy to sing, but the accompaniments are not easy to sight-read. We expect that musicians would practice these accompaniments with the same care they devote to a prelude, postlude, or anthem. Once musicians have mastered a particular hymn they will discover that the setting assiduously prepares the melodic line for the congregation and supplies a sense of vital energy through moving inner voices.

If there is a choir or a small group of singers available to assist in the teaching, take adequate time to work with them on the new selection. Observing the points at which this smaller group has difficulty learning the music will help you to identify the places that will be challenging to the congregation.

We use two methods of introducing new hymns. The first method is adequate in most cases, but when there is a particularly challenging spot, as in "Glory to God Is the Song of Stars" and "Ask, Seek, Knock," we employ the second method. And sometimes, depending on the time and resources available to us, we use both together.

First Method

1. The musician plays the hymn once through on the keyboard.
2. A soloist or the choir sings the first stanza for the congregation.
3. A soloist or the choir sings the second stanza for the congregation while the congregation hums the tune.
4. The congregation joins in singing the remaining stanzas.

Second Method

This is the step-by-step process which we presented in our first book of hymns, *New Hymns for the Lectionary: To Glorify the Maker's Name* (Oxford University Press, 1986).

1. In preparation for the presentation to the congregation, choose a limited portion to discuss which holds special interest or special difficulty for singers.
2. Stand before the people, and begin your presentation with a sentence or two about the overall nature of the hymn.
3. Mention the unusual section and play it (or have the small group sing it).
4. Invite the congregation to sing it.
5. Repeat the demonstration if the congregation has not been able to sing it well, and have them try singing it again.

It is important to have them succeed in singing the challenging section before ending this rehearsal, for they should be able to sing the hymn in its entirety during the worship service without the distractions of a sense of insecurity at the point of rhythmic notation or a melodic interval that is difficult to read.

If there is no small group within the congregation that is able to assist in introducing new music, or if the music leader has no opportunity to teach the people, it may be possible to introduce the tune by playing it several times as a prelude to the service, adding brief interludes between repetitions.

The authority with which the setting is given out at the time the congregation sings is greatly significant in the introduction of any new hymn. Secure, steady, and expressive playing is essential. Bringing out the melody will both clarify its contours and allow those who are preparing to sing the melody to hear the instrument's lyrical presentation as an example.

USING OLDER SETTINGS AS A STEP
TOWARD NEW MUSIC

Because it is sometimes necessary to lead people gently toward acquiring new tastes, several of the texts that have new settings are written in traditional meters so that they may also be sung to established tunes. Not every new text will fit smoothly with a familiar setting. Therefore, if you want to use a traditional setting be sure to try all the stanzas to the setting you choose.

If you start by singing the hymn texts in this book to older settings, do not cheat your congregation by stopping where you begin. The new settings have been composed specifically to heighten the meaning of the texts, and the full impact of these hymns rests in the integration of word and music. So plan carefully, practice thoroughly, and move onward to the new music.

NURTURING THE LIFE OF THE CHURCH

We know it is worth the energy and time that such careful preparation requires. We might compare the process to fixing a meal. Fast food is a convenience, but its flavor and nutrition do not compare with the fresh ingredients of a well-balanced, home-cooked meal. In a similar fashion, congregational song that is instantly accessible does not provide the nurture of a more challenging hymnody. Significant spiritual growth never comes cheaply, and that is as true of congregational song as it is of any other part of the church's life.

Do not limit the introduction of new hymns to Sunday services. There are many other occasions in the life of the church that are appropriate, such as retreats, prayer fellowships, conferences, church suppers, board meetings, and study groups. After people have learned a hymn on one of these less formal occasions, they may be eager to see it become part ot the regular Sunday repertoire.

Consider, also, the use of these hymns as solos or anthems for small church choirs. We were delighted after the publication of our first hymnal to receive tapes of children's choirs and soloists who introduced the new settings to their congregations. By writing or calling the publisher (see the copyright page) you can receive permission to reprint the poetry in your church bulletin to help listeners easily follow the words. This can be particularly effective if the pastor preaches about a topic that is the subject of one of these hymns.

STORIES BEHIND THE HYMNS

Because it is often helpful to know something of the story behind a hymn, we have included such information before the indexes at the end of this book. Perusing these stories, the reader will discover that most of our hymns were commissioned by congregations hungering for new words and music to express their concerns to God. Our hymns grow out of the life of the church and are intended to nurture the life of the church as it celebrates great occasions, cares for its members, and responds to the needs of the world.

We offer this book trusting that in its prayerful use you will discover, as we have, the truth of Jesus' inquiring spirit:

> Ask,
> seek,
> knock.
> Doors that doubt has left untried
> Searching faith can open wide.

Rochester, New York   C. D.
Denver, Colorado   T. H. T.
March 1992

I LIFE CYCLE NEEDS

the care of children

1. Our Savior's Infant Cries Were Heard

baptism, confirmation, reaffirmation of faith

2. If all You Want, Lord, Is My Heart
3, What King Would Wade Through Murky Streams

education

4. Praise the Source of Faith and Learning

marriage

5. We Need Each Other's Voice to Sing

dying

6. Risen Christ, May Death be Swift

grief

7. How Long, O Lord, How Long?

1. Our Savior's Infant Cries Were Heard

(tune: Lullaby)

THOMAS H. TROEGER

CAROL DORAN

1. Our sav-ior's in-fant cries were heard And met by hu-man
2. In Jo-seph's arms, at Mar-y's breast, While Her-od's vio-lence
3. By trust-ing Christ to hu-man care God blessed for-ev-er-
4. Who-ev-er calms a child by night Or guides a youth by
5. For Christ who was a ref-u-gee From Her-od and his

love Be-fore he preached one sav-ing word Or prayed to God a-bove.
2. spread, God's love by hu-man love was blessed, Pro-tect-ed, nur-tured, fed.
more The care of chil-dren ev-ery-where— The bruised, the lost, the poor.
4. day Serves him whose birth by lan-tern light Was on a bed of hay.
sword Is seek-ing now through us to be Our chil-dren's friend and Lord.

Based on Matthew 2:13-23

1. Our Savior's Infant Cries Were Heard

(tune: Lullaby)

CAROL DORAN

2. If all You Want, Lord, Is My Heart

(tune: First Command)

THOMAS H. TROEGER

CAROL DORAN

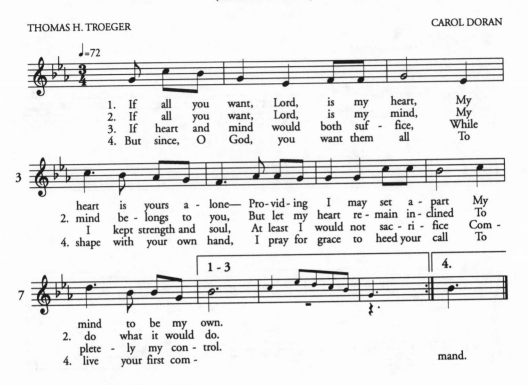

1. If all you want, Lord, is my heart, My
2. If all you want, Lord, is my mind, My
3. If heart and mind would both suf - fice, While
4. But since, O God, you want them all To

heart is yours a - lone— Pro-vid-ing I may set a - part My
2. mind be - longs to you, But let my heart re - main in - clined To
   I kept strength and soul, At least I would not sac - ri - fice Com -
4. shape with your own hand, I pray for grace to heed your call To

mind to be my own.
2. do what it would do.
   plete - ly my con - trol.
4. live your first com - mand.

Based on Deuteronomy 6:4-5
Mark 12:29-30

2. If all You Want, Lord, Is My Heart

(tune: First Command)

CAROL DORAN

3. What King Would Wade Through Murky Streams

(tune: Baptism)

THOMAS H. TROEGER

CAROL DORAN

1. What king would wade through murk - y streams And __ bow be - neath the
2. Christ gleams with wa - ter __ brown with clay From __ land the proph-ets
3. Come bow with Christ be - neath the wave. He __ stands here at your

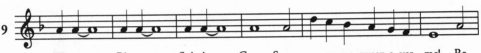

wave, Ig - nor - ing how the world es - teems The pow - er - ful and brave?
2. trod. A - bove him while the clouds give way De - scends the dove of God.
side And rais - es you as from the grave God raised him cru - ci - fied.

Wa - ter, __ Riv - er, __ Spir - it, __ Grace, Sweep o - ver me, sweep o - ver me! Re -

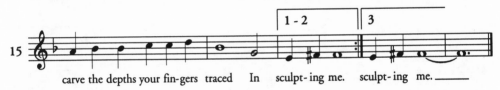

| 1 - 2 | 3 |

carve the depths your fin-gers traced In sculpt-ing me. sculpt-ing me. __

Based on Matthew 3:13-17

3. What King Would Wade Through Murky Streams

(tune: Baptism)

CAROL DORAN

4. Praise the Source of Faith and Learning

(tune: Waldo Beach)

THOMAS H. TROEGER

CAROL DORAN

1. Praise the source of faith and learn-ing Who has sparked and stoked the
2. God of wis-dom, we ac-knowl-edge That our sci-ence and our
3. May our faith re-deem the blun-der Of be-liev-ing that our
4. As two cur-rents in a riv-er Fight each oth-ers' un-der-

mind With a pas-sion for dis-cern-ing How the world has been de-
2. art And the breadth of hu-man knowl-edge On-ly par-tial truth im-
thought Has dis-placed the grounds for won-der Which the an-cient proph-ets
4. tow 'Til con-verg-ing they de-liv-er One co-her-ent stead-y

signed. Let the sense of won-der flow-ing From the won-ders we sur-
2. part. Far be-yond our cal-cu-la-tion Lies a depth we can-not
taught. May our learn-ing curb the er-ror Which un-think-ing faith can
4. flow. Blend, O God, our faith and learn-ing 'Til they carve a sin-gle

vey Keep our faith for-ev-er grow-ing And re-new our need to pray:
2. sound Where your pur-pose for cre-a-tion And the pulse of life are found.
breed Lest we jus-ti-fy some ter-ror With an an-ti-quat-ed creed.
4. course While they join as one re-turn-ing Praise and thanks to you their source.

Based on Proverbs 2:6

4. Praise the Source of Faith and Learning

(tune: Waldo Beach)

CAROL DORAN

5. We Need Each Other's Voice to Sing

(tune: Wedding Gift)
(for J.A. and J.M.B.)

THOMAS H. TROEGER

CAROL DORAN

♩=104

1. We need each oth-er's voice to sing The songs our hearts would raise To
2. We need each oth-er's strength to lift The cross we're called to bear. Each
3. We need each oth-er's views to see The lim-its of the mind, That
4. We need each oth-er's voice to sing, Each oth-er's strength to love, Each

set the whole world ech-o-ing With one great hymn of praise. We
2. oth-er's pres-ence is a gift Of God's in-car-nate care. When
God in fact turns out to be Far more than we've de-fined, That
4. oth-er's views to help us bring Our hearts to God a-bove. Our

blend our voic-es to com-plete the mel-o-dy that starts With
2. acts of love and ten-der speech Con-vey the sav-ior's voice, Then
God's one im-age shines in all, In ev-ery class and race, And
4. lives, like coals placed side by side To feed each oth-er's flame, Shall

God who sets and keeps the beat That stirs our lov-ing hearts.
2. praise ex-ceeds what words can reach And we with song re-joice: We
ev-ery group re-ceives the call To sing with faith and grace:
4. with the Spir-it's breath pro-vide A blaze of faith to claim:

give our al-le-lu-ias to the church-'s com-mon chord: Al-le-

Praise!

lu-ia! Al-le-lu-ia! Praise: O praise, O praise the Lord!

Based on Ephesians 5:19,20

5. We Need Each Other's Voice to Sing

(tune: Wedding Gift)
(for J.A. and J.M.B.)

CAROL DORAN

6. Risen Christ, May Death be Swift

(tune: Jansje)

THOMAS H. TROEGER

CAROL DORAN

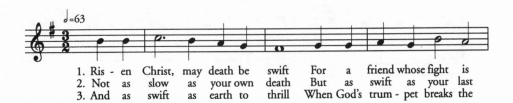

1. Ris - en Christ, may death be swift For a friend whose fight is
2. Not as slow as your own death But as swift as your last
3. And as swift as earth to thrill When God's trum - pet breaks the

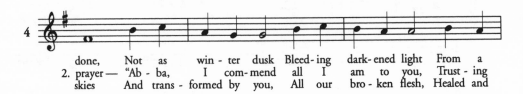

done, Not as win - ter dusk Bleed - ing dark-ened light From a
2. prayer— "Ab - ba, I com- mend all I am to you, Trust - ing
skies And trans - formed by you, All our bro - ken flesh, Healed and

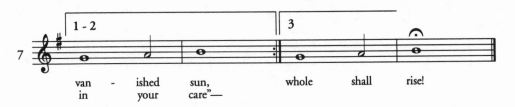

1 - 2
van - ished sun,
in your care"—

3
whole shall rise!

Based on I Corinthians 15:50-55
Luke 23:46

6. Risen Christ, May Death be Swift

(tune: Jansje)

CAROL DORAN

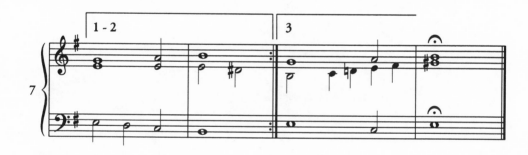

7. How Long, O Lord, How Long?

(tune: Lament)

THOMAS H. TROEGER

CAROL DORAN

1. How long, O Lord, how long? The an - cient cry is ours. We
2. And why, O Lord, and why? We ask with ev - ery age And
3. The cross, O Lord, the cross! We think a - bout your son: You
4. Your hand, O Lord, your hand! We need your hand to hold, To
5. We trust, O Lord, we trust In time our grief shall mend. Trans -

   wait in grief and ask how long Be - fore we feel your powers.
2. throw a - gainst your dis - tant sky The force of grief and rage.
   know the weight and edge of loss, Your tears and ours are one.
4. walk this dark, un - chart - ed land Where sol - id mean - ings fold.
   formed by love that shaped our dust, Your love that knows no end.

Based on Psalm 13

7. How Long, O Lord, How Long?

(tune: Lament)

CAROL DORAN

II SPECIAL CONGREGATIONAL NEEDS

celebrating ministries of music

8. *Glory to God Is the Song of the Stars*
9. *Make Your Prayer and Music One*

celebrating ministries of the word

10. *The Rocks Would Shout if We Kept Still*

confession and renewal

11. *The Cross on the Hill Is the Measuring Rod*

spiritual discipline

12. *Eagles' Spiralings Comply*
13. *Let all Who Pray the Prayer Christ Taught*
14. *Through Our Fragmentary Prayers*

ordination, commissioning, installation, consecration

15. *Pastor, Lead Our Circle Dance*

church anniversaries and rededications

16. *We Travel Toward a Land Unknown*
17. *View the Present Through the Promise*

8. Glory to God Is the Song of the Stars

(tune: Branches)

THOMAS H. TROEGER

CAROL DORAN

1. Glo - ry to God is the song of the stars,
2. Dawn gives the song of the stars to the sun.
3. Light that's re - call - ing the light in our hearts
4. Sing with the si - lence of stars and the sun,

Mu - sic so deep that the si - lence is sound, Mu - sic too
2. Watch - ing its bright - ness suf - fus - ing the skies, We with the
Falls on the leaves that are feed - ing the vine, Swells the round
4. Sing by pro - vid - ing for all to be fed, Sing through your

lyr - ic for me - ter and bars, Flow - ing as prayer that no
2. psalm - ist re - mem - ber the One Who with com - pas - sion and
fruit with the praise it im - parts, Praise we re - lease when we
4. ac - tions so jus - tice is done, Sing through your deeds that the

lan - guage has bound, Gath - er - ing out of the reach - es of
2. jus - tice sup - plies Wis - dom that shines through com - mand - ment and
pour out the wine, Sing - ing that Christ is the vine that we
4. gos - pel may spread. Then when you sing with the sound of your

Broadening

space Meas - ure - less prais - es of in - fi - nite grace:
2. law Wak - ing in us our thanks - giv - ing and awe:
share, Branch - es he feeds through our wor - ship and prayer:
4. voice, Earth as one cho - rus will sing and re - joice:

Refrain

♩=120

Glory, glory, glo - ry to God! All of cre - a - tion sings ad - o - ra - tion.

| 1, 2, 3 | Tempo I |
| 4 |

Glory, glory, glo - ry to God!

God!

Based on Psalm 19:1-10
Based on John 15:1-5

© 1987, Carol Doran and Thomas H. Troeger

19

8. Glory to God Is the Song of the Stars

(tune: Branches)

CAROL DORAN

© 1987, Carol Doran and Thomas H. Troeger

9. Make Your Prayer and Music One

(tune: Faithful Songs)

THOMAS H. TROEGER

CAROL DORAN

Based on Acts 16:25

9. Make Your Prayer and Music One

(tune: Faithful Songs)

CAROL DORAN

10. The Rocks Would Shout if We Kept Still

(tune: Preachers)

THOMAS H. TROEGER

CAROL DORAN

Based on Luke 20:40

10. The Rocks Would Shout if We Kept Still

(tune: Preachers)

CAROL DORAN

11. The Cross on the Hill Is the Measuring Rod

(tune: Measuring Rod)

THOMAS H. TROEGER

CAROL DORAN

1. The cross on the hill is the meas-ur-ing rod That
2. We hold up our lives to the cross on the hill And
3. O Christ, we are stunned by the span of our sin That

plumbs to the lim-it our sin and pre-ten-sion, And
2. trace in our his-tory the trag-ic de-clen-sion Of
shad-ows our knowl-edge, our art and in-ven-tion, But

marks where they meet that pro-found-er di-men-sion: The
2. just-ice and love and our fin-est in-ten-tion To
thanks to your grace that is past com-pre-hen-sion New

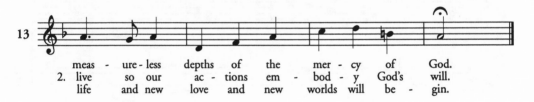

meas - ure-less depths of the mer-cy of God.
2. live so our ac-tions em-bod-y God's will.
life and new love and new worlds will be-gin.

Based on I Corinthians 1:18-25

11. The Cross on the Hill Is the Measuring Rod

(tune: Measuring Rod)

CAROL DORAN

12. Eagles' Spiralings Comply

(tune: Freedom)

THOMAS H. TROEGER   CAROL DORAN

1. Ea - gles' spi - ral - ings com - ply   To the den - si - ties of   sky   And the
2. Lord, you made earth's i - ron   core   And the hol - low bone and   wind,   And you
3. In our mus - cle and our bone   What the ea - gle knows is   known. Help the

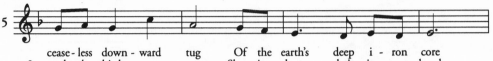

   cease - less down - ward   tug   Of the earth's   deep   i - ron   core
2. taught the birds   to   soar,   Show - ing how   their wings must bend
   heart now, Lord,   to   learn   That the   free - dom it de - sires,

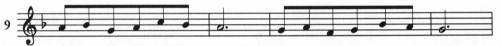

   And what lig - a - ments can   bear   Tens - ing flesh and hol - low   bone
2. For the mass and speed and   force   Of the air to   lift their weight
   Like all soar - ing flight, re - quires   That we bend our strength and   skill

Refrain

   Stiff a - gainst the rush of   air.
2. As they glide and carve their course.   Cir - cling,   cir - cling,   Swoop - ing,
   To your word and wind and   will.

   Plan - ing,   Ris - ing,   ris - ing   Heav - en   gain - ing.

Based on John 8:32
  I Peter 2:16

12. Eagles' Spiralings Comply

(tune: Freedom)

CAROL DORAN

13. Let all Who Pray the Prayer Christ Taught

(tune: Ambrose Swasey)

THOMAS H. TROEGER

CAROL DORAN

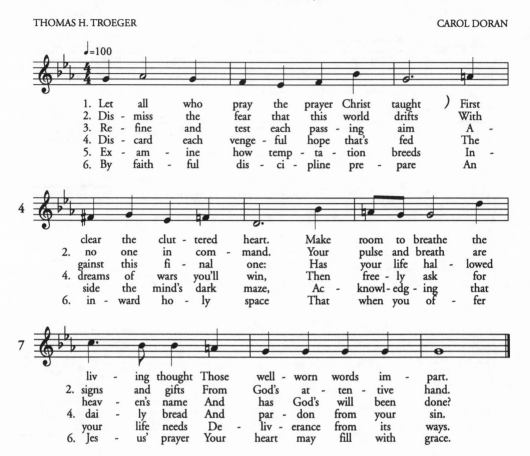

1. Let all who pray the prayer Christ taught) First clear the cluttered heart. Make room to breathe the living thought Those well-worn words impart.
2. Dismiss the fear that this world drifts With no one in command. Your pulse and breath are signs and gifts From God's attentive hand.
3. Refine and test each passing aim Against this final one: Has your life hallowed heaven's name And has God's will been done?
4. Discard each vengeful hope that's fed The dreams of wars you'll win, Then freely ask for daily bread And pardon from your sin.
5. Examine how temptation breeds In the mind's dark maze, Acknowledging that your life needs Deliverance from its ways.
6. By faithful discipline prepare An inward holy space That when you offer Jesus' prayer Your heart may fill with grace.

Based on Matthew 6:7-15

13. Let all Who Pray the Prayer Christ Taught

(tune: Ambrose Swasey)

CAROL DORAN

14. Through Our Fragmentary Prayers

(tune: Wordless)

THOMAS H. TROEGER

CAROL DORAN

1. Through our frag-men-tar - y prayers   And our si - lent heart-hid sighs
2. Deep - er than the pulse-'s   beat   Is the Spir - it's speech-less groan,
3. *Let our jab - ber-ings give way   To the hum-mings in the soul
4. Search and sound our mind and heart,   Breath and Flame and Wind and Dove,

  Word-less - ly the Spir - it bears Our pro-found-est needs and cries:
2. Mak- ing hu - man prayers com-plete Through the prayer that is God's own.
  As we yield our lives this day To the God who makes us whole:
4. Let your prayer in us im - part Strength to do the work of love.

Hum (or Ah) _____
**Alleluia, alleluia, alleluia,

*Verse 3 optional.
**Alleluias optional for final verse. Sing in free rhythm.

Based on Romans 8:26-27

14. Through Our Fragmentary Prayers

(tune: Wordless)

CAROL DORAN

15. Pastor,* Lead Our Circle Dance

(tune: Rockwell)

For the Rt. Reverend Hays Rockwell, on the occasion of his Ordination and Consecration
as Bishop Coadjutor of the Diocese of Missouri, March 2, 1991.

THOMAS H. TROEGER

CAROL DORAN

1. Pas - tor, lead our cir - cle dance which the Spir - it has be - gun,
2. From the cen - ter lead and show steps and leaps we nev - er tried,
3. If the cir - cle gets too tight stop the dance and don't be - gin
4. Pas - tor, lead our cir - cle dance as the Spir - it leads and calls

help us hand in hand ad-vance, show us how to move as
2. then al - low the dance to flow, danc - ing with us side by
'til our o - pen hands in - vite all whom Je - sus wel - comes
4. 'til the cir - cle's whole ex-panse moves be - yond our bounds and

one. Some de - mand a driv-ing beat, oth - ers ask to slow the pace.
2. side. Let each danc - er take a turn, danc-ing in the cen - ter free
in. For the dance of faith be-longs to the strang-ers in the street,
4. walls And we dance with dis - tant suns danc-ing in the dark a - bove,

Teach us how to bend and meet our con - flict- ed needs with grace.
2. so that all can teach and learn what our cir - cle dance could be.
and we need their steps and songs for the dance to be com - plete.
4. danc - ing as cre - a - tion runs on the en - er - gies of love.

* Bishop, Deacon, Rector, Elder, Teacher, etc.

Based on II Samuel 6:14-15

34

15. Pastor, Lead Our Circle Dance

(tune: Rockwell)

CAROL DORAN

16. We Travel Toward a Land Unknown

(tune: Adventure)

THOMAS H. TROEGER

CAROL DORAN

1. We trav - el toward a land un-known, God's word our on - ly
2. Then where our free-dom first was won We set - tle down to
3. And when we think the jour-ney's end Is ver - y near at
4. We trav - el toward a land un-known, But all a - long the

chart, And breathe in the wind that has swept and blown From that
2. stay, But find that the jour - ney has just be - gun And the
hand We learn that the road has an - oth - er bend And we're
4. route We're thank - ing our Lord for the won - ders shown And the

land to the hu - man heart, And on the wind_____ we
2. wind blows an - oth - er way, And on the wind_____ we
far from the prom - ised land, But then the wind_____ re -
4. faith that has con - quered doubt. Give thanks the wind_____ is

hear the sound Of Mir - i - am's dance by the sea, And we
2. hear the song Of Mo - ses and Da - vid and Ruth, Who are
turns and lifts Our heart and our strength and our soul, And we're
4. blow - ing still, And pray that the church may be blessed With the

dance with the slaves whom Phar - aoh bound But the Lord of hosts set free.
2. giv - ing us strength to right the wrong And to speak and do the truth.
filled with the stead - fast Christ-like gifts That re - veal a - gain our goal.
4. vis - ion and grace to do God's will And be faith - ful on its quest.

Based on Genesis 12:1-3

16. We Travel Toward a Land Unknown

(tune: Adventure)

CAROL DORAN

17. View the Present Through the Promise

(tune: Homiletics)

THOMAS H. TROEGER

CAROL DORAN

1. View the pres-ent through the prom-ise Christ will come a - gain.
2. Probe the pres-ent with the prom-ise Christ will come a - gain.
3. Match the pres-ent to the prom-ise Christ will come a - gain.

Trust des-pite the deep-ening dark-ness Christ will come a - gain.
2. Let your dai-ly ac-tions wit-ness Christ will come a - gain.
Make this hope your guid-ing prem-ise Christ will come a - gain.

Lift the world a-bove its griev-ing Through your watch-ing and be-liev-ing
2. Let your lov-ing and your giv-ing And your jus-tice and for-giv-ing
Pat-tern all your cal-cu-lat-ing And the world you are cre-at-ing

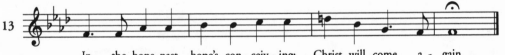

In the hope past hope's con-ceiv-ing: Christ will come a - gain.
2. Be a sign to all the liv-ing: Christ will come a - gain.
To the ad-vent you are wait-ing: Christ will come a - gain.

Based on Matthew 24:42-44

17. View the Present Through the Promise

(tune: Homiletics)

CAROL DORAN

III THEOLOGICAL AND SOCIAL NEEDS

victims of abuse

18. *Holy and Good Is the Gift of Desire*

different kinds of families

19. *God Made from One Blood all the Families of Earth*

inclusive images for God

20. *Source and Sovereign, Rock and Cloud*

the search for faith

21. *Ask, Seek, Knock*
22. *When There Is No Star to Guide You*

the search for justice

23. *The Least in God's Kingdom Is Greater than John*

the search for peace

24. *Fierce the Force that Curled Cain's Fist*
25. *Lions and Oxen Will Feed in the Hay*

18. Holy and Good Is the Gift of Desire

(tune: Poling)

THOMAS H. TROEGER

CAROL DORAN

18. Holy and Good Is the Gift of Desire

(tune: Poling)

CAROL DORAN

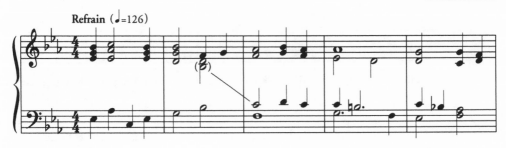

To stanzas 1, 2, 3 | After stanza 3

rit.

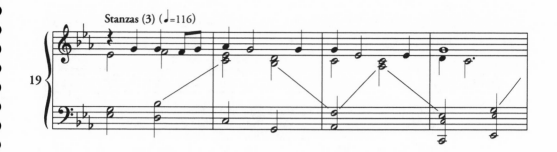

19. God Made from One Blood all the Families of Earth

(tune: Families)

THOMAS H. TROEGER

CAROL DORAN

1. God made from one blood all the fam-ilies of earth,
2. We turn to you, God, with our thanks and our tears
3. We learn through fam-ilies how our close-ness and trust
4. Give, Lord, each fam-ily lost in con-flict and storm
5. Make wide that wis-dom and that grace to in-clude

The cir-cles of nur-ture that raised us from birth, Com-
2. For all of the fam-ilies we've known through the years, The
In-crease when our ac-tions are lov-ing and just. Yet
4. A sense of your wis-dom and grace that trans-form Sharp
The rac-es and view-points our fam-ilies ex-clude 'Til

pan-ions who join us to walk through each stage Of
2. in-ti-mate net-works on whom we de-pend Of
fam-ilies have al-so dis-tort-ed their roles, Mis-
4. an-ger to in-sight which strength-ens the heart And
peace in each home bears and nur-tures the bud Of

child-hood and youth and a-dult-hood and age.
2. par-ent and part-ner and room-mate and friend.
treat-ing their mem-bers and bruis-ing their souls.
4. makes clear the place where re-build-ing can start.
peace shared by all you have made from one blood.

Based on Acts 17:26
Ephesians 3:14-15

© 1989, 1991 Oxford University Press, Inc.

19. God Made from One Blood all the Families of Earth

(tune: Families)

CAROL DORAN

20. Source and Sovereign, Rock and Cloud

(tune: God's Names)

THOMAS H. TROEGER

CAROL DORAN

1. Source and Sov-ereign, Rock and Cloud, For-tress, Foun-tain,
2. Word and Wis-dom, Root and Vine, Shep-herd, Sav-ior,
3. Storm and Still-ness, Breath and Dove, Thun-der, Tem-pest,

Shel-ter, Light, Judge, De-fen-der, Mer-cy, Might,
2. Ser-vant, Lamb, Well and Wa-ter, Bread and Wine,
Whirl-wind, Fire, Com-fort, Coun-selor, Pres-ence, Love

Life whose life all life en-dowed:
2. Way who leads us to I AM:
En-er-gies that nev-er tire:

Refrain

May the church at prayer re-call That no sin-gle, ho-ly name But the truth that feeds them all Is the God whom we pro-claim.

Based on Exodus 3:13-14

20. Source and Sovereign, Rock and Cloud

(tune: God's Names)

CAROL DORAN

21. Ask, Seek, Knock

(tune: Open Door)

THOMAS H. TROEGER

CAROL DORAN

Based on Matthew 7:7-12

21. Ask, Seek, Knock

(tune: Open Door)

CAROL DORAN

22. When There Is No Star to Guide You

(tune: Convocation)

THOMAS H. TROEGER

CAROL DORAN

1. When there is no star to guide you and you can-not wait for day and your
2. Be a - lert to shifts in weath - er: if it turns to cold and frost hud - dle
3. If you think you have dis - cov - ered with your lan-tern in the night some clear
4. You may some-times trip and stum - ble on a hid-den root or stone but re -

an - cient maps pro - vide you on - ly hints to find the way,
2. close - ly all to - geth - er, check if an - y have been lost.
path the dark has cov - ered let the oth - ers bring their light.
4. mem - ber as you grum - ble that you do not fall a - lone.

keep with-in each oth-er's call - ing, Mark each time you make a turn,
2. Lis - ten for a riv-er flow - ing, feel for damp - er mov-ing air,
Test your sin-gle lone per-cep - tion in their gath - ered shin-ing beams,
4. And in risk-ing dark ex-pan - ses nev - er marked on map or chart

Broadening

shout for help if you are fall - ing, tell each oth - er all you learn.
2. trace from where the wind is blow - ing, move on brave-ly but with care.
what you saw may be pro - jec - tion fed by shad-ows, fears, and dreams.
4. you will find that faith ad - vanc - es through the land-scape of your heart.

Based on II Corinthians 5:7

22. When There Is No Star to Guide You

(tune: Convocation)

CAROL DORAN

23. The Least in God's Kingdom Is Greater than John

(tune: Cranberry Lake)

THOMAS H. TROEGER

CAROL DORAN

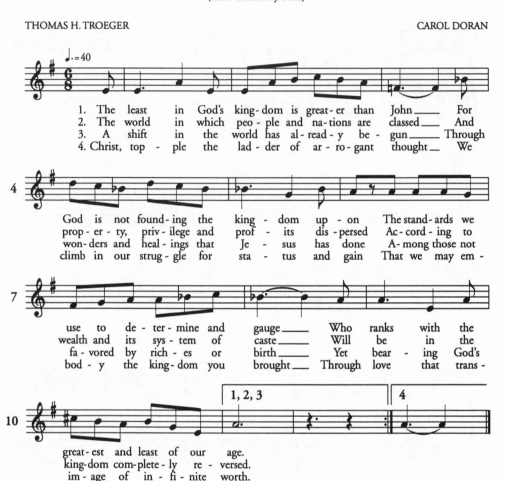

1. The least in God's king-dom is great-er than John____ For God is not found-ing the king - dom up - on The stand-ards we use to de - ter - mine and gauge____ Who ranks with the great-est and least of our age.
2. The world in which peo - ple and na-tions are classed____ And prop - er - ty, priv - ilege and prof - its dis -persed Ac-cord-ing to wealth and its sys - tem of caste____ Will be in the king-dom com-plete-ly re - versed.
3. A shift in the world has al - read - y be - gun____ Through won-ders and heal - ings that Je - sus has done A-mong those not fa - vored by rich - es or birth____ Yet bear - ing God's im - age of in - fi - nite worth.
4. Christ, top - ple the lad - der of ar - ro - gant thought__ We climb in our strug - gle for sta - tus and gain That we may em - bod - y the king-dom you brought__ Through love that trans - fig - ures in - jus - tice and pain. ____

1, 2, 3

4

Based on Luke 7:28

23. The Least in God's Kingdom Is Greater than John

(tune: Cranberry Lake)

CAROL DORAN

24. Fierce the Force that Curled Cain's Fist

(tune: Heaven's Peace)

THOMAS H. TROEGER

CAROL DORAN

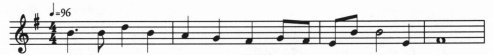

1. Fierce the force that curled Cain's fist— Would he mas-ter it or yield?
2. A-bel's blood is cry-ing still, Cry-ing, cry-ing from the ground
3. Ev-ery fist an o-pen hand, Ev-ery sword a prun-er's blade,
4. We con-fess we are Cain's heirs, That the vio-lent heart is ours

Thick the bit-ter weep-ing mist Ris-ing from the red-dened field.
2. While the heirs of Cain yet kill And the pleas of earth are drowned.
Ev-ery bomb in ev-ery land To a plow or trac-tor made,
4. And that mas-tered by our fears We suc-cumb to le-thal powers,

Broadly (♩=60)

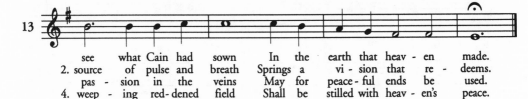

God whose love for love a-lone Shaped us deep in E-den's shade, Wept to
2. But the hearts that fash-ion death Beat as well with ho-ly dreams— From the
Ev-ery rag-ing soul like Cain's With the grace of God in-fused That the
4. Yet this day we shall not yield, For by grace we'll seek re-lease 'Til the

see what Cain had sown In the earth that heav-en made.
2. source of pulse and breath Springs a vi-sion that re-deems.
pas-sion in the veins May for peace-ful ends be used.
4. weep-ing red-dened field Shall be stilled with heav-en's peace.

Based on Genesis 4:1-15

24. Fierce the Force that Curled Cain's Fist

(tune: Heaven's Peace)

CAROL DORAN

25. Lions and Oxen Will Feed in the Hay

(tune: Isaiah's Dream)

THOMAS H. TROEGER

CAROL DORAN

♩=100

1. Li - ons and ox - en will feed in the hay, Leo - pards will
2. Peace will per - vade more than for - est and field: God will trans -
3. Na - ture re - or - dered to match God's in - tent, Na - tions o -

join with the lambs as they play, Wolves will be pas - tured with
2. fig - ure the vio - lence con - cealed Deep in the heart and in
bey - ing the call to re - pent, All of cre - a - tion com -

cows in the glade— Blood will not dark - en the earth that God
2. sys - tems of gain, Ripe for the judg - ment the Lord will or -
plete - ly re - stored, Filled with the knowl - edge and love of the

made.
2. dain. Lit - tle child whose bed is straw, Take new lodg-ings in my heart.
Lord!

Bring the dream I - sai - ah saw:
1. Life re - deemed from fang and claw.
2. Just - ice pur - i - fy - ing law.
3. Knowl - edge, wis - dom, wor - ship, awe.

Based on Isaiah 11:1-10
Luke 2:7

25. Lions and Oxen Will Feed in the Hay

(tune: Isaiah's Dream)

CAROL DORAN

NOTES

1. Our Savior's Infant Cries Were Heard
Commissioned in 1986 by Barium Springs Home for Children in Barium Springs, North Carolina, in anticipation of their centennial celebration in 1991. The home provides a number of programs to serve children, youth, and families needing help. They wanted a hymn about the care of children that would "be useful as a gift to the church from our celebration." The hymn is appropriate not only for Christmas, but for any occasion celebrating the care and nurture of children.

2. If all You Want, Lord, Is My Heart
Inspired by George Herbert's poetry and a number of our workshops in which we examined the issue of how to use all that we are in the service and worship of God. The tune suddenly moves from E flat major to C minor at the moment where we acknowledge our unwillingness to give all to God. The music is thus aiding the process of spiritual realization that the text articulates.

3. What King Would Wade Through Murky Streams
Written at the request of many pastors, seminary students, and users of our first book of hymns who asked that we provide in our next volume a hymn on the baptism of Christ. The music, like the poetry, changes character at the refrain in order to lead the congregation toward a sense of the sweeping, flowing action of God upon their lives.

4. Praise the Source of Faith and Learning
Commissioned by Duke University with the stipulation that the hymn should be on the school's motto, "Faith and Learning." The commission was supported by a fund named after Waldo Beach, Professor Emeritus of Christian Ethics at Duke University Divinity School.

5. We Need Each Other's Voice to Sing
Commissioned as a wedding gift for Jan Anderson and J. Melvin Butler by the choir of the Downtown United Presbyterian Church in Rochester, New York, when Dr. Butler was organist and choir director at the church. Representatives of the choir requested a hymn that would be appropriate for the wedding and also be usable on other occasions when the church is affirming its corporate life together. The descant on the final line of the refrain can make this hymn especially stirring.

6. Risen Christ, May Death be Swift
Written when a close friend and colleague was in the last hours of her life. The tune, Jansje, is named for her. The simple melody is meant to provide instant accessibility for people whose sorrow would make it too taxing to learn anything more difficult. We hope this hymn helps people express the prayer of their hearts when there is nothing left to do but pray that a loved one may find release through death.

7. How Long, O Lord, How Long?

Inspired by Psalm 13 and our awareness that many grieving people find their ability to pray blocked because they have not been given permission to express their anger and sense of abandonment. We hope the simple setting will make this easily usable for funerals and memorial services.

8. Glory to God Is the Song of the Stars

Commissioned in 1987 by St. Thomas Episcopal Church, Rochester, New York, for the dedication of a new organ. We were asked to create a text drawing on Psalm 19 and John 15:1a ("I am the true vine"). This image bears special meaning for the church because a vine is carved into the wooden cross above its chancel. The request was for a "big hymn with a big refrain" that would employ the riches of the new instrument and that could be used on other festive occasions.

9. Make Your Prayer and Music One

Inspired by one of our former colleagues, Gayraud Wilmore, who related the songs of oppressed African Americans to Acts 16:25: "But about midnight Paul and Silas were praying and singing hymns to God, and the prisoners were listening to them."

10. The Rocks Would Shout if We Kept Still

Commissioned by the Academy of Homiletics, a scholarly guild of those who teach preaching in the theological schools of Canada and the United States, in celebration of their twenty-fifth anniversary, December 1990. For a number of years both composer and poet were responsible for organizing and leading worship at the academy's annual meetings.

11. The Cross on the Hill Is the Measuring Rod

Written to address the dissonance in our community between the love and justice we proclaim and the actuality of our lives.

12. Eagles' Spiralings Comply

Written after hearing a surfeit of sermons on freedom that did not acknowledge the place of discipline in liberation. The free flight of the eagle was an image common to many of these sermons, and the hymn is an effort to redeem the maligned bird's reputation. The music of the refrain allows us to enjoy the lift and thrill of flight that results from the careful balance of forces described in the stanzas.

13. Let all Who Pray the Prayer Christ Taught

Requested by the Colgate Rochester school librarian, Norman Kansfield, who took over the editorship of *Rejoice in the Lord* after Eric Routley died. He thought the hymnal might need another text on the Lord's Prayer. That turned out not to be the case, and the hymn appeared instead in a small collection entitled *New Songs of Praise 2* (Oxford: Oxford University Press, 1986). The hymn is intended to help people pray the Lord's Prayer with a renewed sense of its meaning.

14. Through Our Fragmentary Prayers

An experimental piece in which the music intones the mysterious spiritual process described by the text. The setting combines the vigor of metrical hymnody with an opportunity to sense the wordless motions of the Spirit stirring us to prayer.

During the refrain following the final stanza, people may repeat on the sustained note simple exclamations of prayer without doing them to any particular rhythm.

15. Pastor, Lead Our Circle Dance

Written as a gift for Hays Rockwell, a friend and colleague and former dean at Colgate Rochester, upon his consecration as a bishop in the Episcopal Church. The image of the circle dance suggests how a leader's role is to draw out the gifts of the entire group, a manner of working with others which we celebrate in our friend's ministry. The hymn was written to be sung by the congregation to the person(s) being ordained, commissioned, consecrated, etc. It is a way for the community to make a musical and liturgical statement about what it hopes for from its leader.

16. We Travel Toward a Land Unknown
Initially written for the Presbyterian bicentennial, "Celebrate the Journey," but appropriate for Pentecost. The word "wind" sung to an eighth note pattern occurs in every stanza at the same point. The hymn would also be helpful on any occasion when the church marks some crucial turning point in its journey of faith.

17. View the Present Through the Promise
Written for a hymn search for new Advent hymns sponsored by the Hymn Society of America in 1986. In the second half of the setting the music climbs to the unexpected D natural to suggest the inexplicable nature of the hymn's repeated promise, "Christ will come again."

18. Holy and Good Is the Gift of Desire
Commissioned by James Poling, our colleague in pastoral theology, who has done extensive theological and psychological research on the sources and nature of violence. (See his book, *The Abuse of Power a Theological Problem* [Abingdon, 1991].) He was going to preach a sermon on what males need to do in face of the devastating history of sexism. We wrote the hymn to follow his sermon, and soon discovered that many groups wanted to use it. This is a dramatic example of how new pastoral concerns awaken new hymns.

19. God Made from One Blood all the Families of Earth
Commissioned by Russell Shultz-Widmar for a collection of hymns for colleges and universities. The request stressed the need for a hymn that would include many kinds of family other than the nuclear. He wanted a hymn that was candid about family life, its liabilities as well as its strengths and values. The opening line was suggested by the King James Version of Acts 17:26: "And hath made of one blood all nations of men for to dwell on all the face of the earth, and hath determined the times before appointed, and the bounds of their habitation." Once the setting was composed, the opening lines of the third, fourth, and fifth stanzas were reworked to match the words more carefully to the strong opening melody.

20. Source and Sovereign, Rock and Cloud
Commissioned by the editorial committee of the new United Methodist hymnal, 1989. They asked for a hymn that would help the church celebrate the diversity of images for God in Scripture and tradition. The lists of images are followed by a refrain intended to remind congregations of the theological importance of addressing God in many different ways.

21. Ask, Seek, Knock
Written in 1986 for Colgate Rochester's annual "Conference on the Ministry," which brings people to campus to consider whether they should attend theological school. The repeated line "Ask, seek, knock," which was the theme of the conference, is based on Matthew 7:7: "Ask, and it will be given you; seek, and you will find; knock and it will be opened to you" (RSV). This is perhaps the most challenging hymn in the book. We suggest it be sung as a responsive hymn between choir and congregation. Have a cantor line out the refrain for the congregation, bringing to their attention the syncopated rhythm on "knock." Then have the choir sing the stanzas with everyone joining in the refrain.

22. When There Is No Star to Guide You
Written to fulfill a request by Colgate Rochester for a "post-modern" hymn for its annual Spring Convocation in 1991, which focused on the theme "Reaching for Values in a Post-Modern Age." The text provides a poetic image of the church facing issues and perspectives that are not always illumined by tradition. The hymn pictures this situation as an occasion for expanding our faith and renewing our sense of mutual interdependence.

23. The Least in God's Kingdom Is Greater than John
Written for no special occasion, but arising instead from the accumulated impact of the liberation theologies that we have read, heard, and discussed during our years in theological education. Each stanza is one continuous sentence. The music shifts from minor to major and back again to reflect the reversals in the text.

24. Fierce the Force that Curled Cain's Fist
Written for a search for peace hymns sponsored by the Hymn Society of America in 1985. The heavy dissonance mirrors the dissonance of the violence described by the poetry.

25. Lions and Oxen Will Feed in the Hay
Inspired by a retired colleague in historical theology, Charles Nielsen, whose Christmas card every year always features some artist's rendering of Isaiah's vision of the peaceable kingdom.

Metrical Index

Hymn number

SHORT METER
S. M. (6-6-8-6)

Lament   7

COMMON METER
C. M. (8-6-8-6)

Lullaby   1
First Command   2
Ambrose Swasey   13

COMMON METER WITH REFRAIN IN COMMON METER

Preachers   10

COMMON METER WITH IRREGULAR REFRAIN

Baptism   3

COMMON METER DOUBLE WITH REFRAIN
C. M. D. (8-6-8-6 D)

Wedding Gift   5

8-5-8-5-8-8-8-5

Homiletics   17

8-6-10-8-8-8-10-7

Adventure   16

Hymn number

7-7-5-5-5

Jansje   6

7-7-7-7 WITH INTERLUDE

Wordless   14

7-7-7-7 WITH ALLELUIAS

Faithful Songs   9

7-7-7-7 D

God's Names   20
Heaven's Peace   24
Rockwell   15

7-7-7-7-7-7-7 WITH REFRAIN

Freedom   12

3-7-7-7-3-7-3-7-7

Open Door   21

8-7-8-7 D

Convocation   22
Waldo Beach   4

Hymn number

10-10-10-10
6-5-6-5-5-5-6-5

    Poling   18

10-10-10-10-7-7-7-7

    Isaiah's Dream   25

10-10-10-10-10-10 WITH REFRAIN,
  8-5-5-8

    Branches   8

Hymn number

11-6-6-5-7-11

    Measuring Rod   11

11-11-11-11

    Families   19
    Cranberry Lake   23

Scriptural Index

Passage	Hymn title	Hymn number
Genesis 1:27-28	Holy and Good Is the Gift of Desire	18
Genesis 4:1-15	Fierce the Force that Curled Cain's Fist	24
Genesis 12:1-3	We Travel Toward a Land Unknown	16
Exodus 3:13-14	Source and Sovereign, Rock and Cloud	20
Deuteronomy 6:4-5	If all You Want, Lord, Is My Heart	2
Samuel 6:14-15	Pastor, Lead Our Circle Dance	15
Psalm 13	How Long, O Lord, How Long?	7
Psalm 19:1-10	Glory to God Is the Song of the Stars	8
Proverbs 2:6	Praise the Source of Faith and Learning	4
Isaiah 11:1-10	Lions and Oxen Will Feed in the Hay	25
Matthew 2:13-23	Our Savior's Infant Cries Were Heard	1
Matthew 3:13-18	What King Would Wade Through Murky Streams	3
Matthew 6:7-15	Let all Who Pray the Prayer Christ Taught	13
Matthew 7:7-12	Ask, Seek, Knock	21
Matthew 24:42-44	View the Present Through the Promise	17
Mark 12:29	If all You Want, Lord, Is My Heart	2
Luke 2:7	Lions and Oxen Will Feed in the Hay	25
Luke 7:28	The Least in God's kingdom Is Greater than John	23
Luke 20:40	The Rocks Would Shout if We Kept Still	10
Luke 23:46	Risen Christ, May Death be Swift	6
John 8:32	Eagles' Spiralings Comply	12
John 15:1-5	Glory to God Is the Song of the Stars	8
Acts 16:25	Make Your Prayer and Music One	9
Acts 17:26	God Made from One Blood all the Families of Earth	19
Romans 8:26-27	Through Our Fragmentary Prayers	14
I Corinthians 1:18-25	The Cross on the Hill Is the Measuring Rod	11
I Corinthians 15:51-52	Risen Christ, May Death be Swift	6
II Corinthians 5:7	When There Is No Star to Guide You	22
Ephesians 3:14-15	God Made from One Blood all the Families of Earth	19
Ephesians 5:19-20	We Need Each Other's Voice to Sing	5
I Peter 2:16	Eagles' Spiralings Comply	12

Index by Pastoral Need, Special Occasion, and Liturgical Season

Hymn number

ABUSED PERSONS

Fierce the Force that Curled Cain's Fist   24
God Made from One Blood all the
    Families of Earth   19
Holy and Good Is the Gift of Desire   18
Our Savior's Infant Cries Were Heard   1

ADVENT

Lions and Oxen Will Feed in the Hay   25
View the Present Through the Promise   17
What King Would Wade Through
    Murky Streams   3

ANNIVERSARY CELEBRATIONS

We Travel Toward a Land Unknown   16

BAPTISM

If all You Want, Lord, Is My Heart   2
What King Would Wade Through
    Murky Streams   3

CALL OF GOD

Ask, Seek, Knock   21

CHILDREN

God Made from One Blood all the
    Families of Earth   19

Hymn number

Lions and Oxen Will Feed in the Hay   25
Our Savior's Infant Cries Were Heard   1

CHRISTMAS

Lions and Oxen Will Feed in the Hay   25
Our Savior's Infant Cries Were Heard   1

CHURCH'S CORPORATE LIFE

Eagles' Spiralings Comply   12
We Need Each Other's Voice to Sing   5
When There Is No Star to Guide You   22

COMMISSIONING

Pastor, Lead Our Circle Dance   15
The Rocks Would Shout if We Kept Still   10
When There Is No Star to Guide You   22

CONFESSION

Fierce the Force that Curled Cain's Fist   24
The Cross on the Hill Is the Measuring
    Rod   11

CONFIRMATION

Ask, Seek, Knock   21
If all You Want, Lord, Is My Heart   2

Hymn number

What King Would Wade Through
Murky Streams   3

CONSECRATION

Pastor, Lead Our Circle Dance   15

CROSS

How Long, O Lord, How Long?   7
The Cross on the Hill Is the Measuring
Rod   11

DEATH

How Long, O Lord, How Long?   7
Risen Christ, May Death be Swift   6

DEDICATIONS

If all You Want, Lord, Is My Heart   2
View the Present Through the Promise   17
We Travel Toward a Land Unkown   16

DYING

Risen Christ, May Death be Swift   6

EASTER

Risen Christ, May Death be Swift   6

EDUCATION

Praise the Source of Faith and Learning   4
When There Is No Star to Guide You   22

EPIPHANY

What King Would Wade Through
Murky Streams   3
When There Is No Star to Guide You   22

EVANGELISM

The Rocks Would Shout if We Kept Still   10

Hymn number

FAITH

Ask, Seek, Knock   21
When There Is No Star to Guide You   22

FAMILIES

God Made from One Blood all the
Families of Earth   19
Holy and Good Is the Gift of Desire   18
Our Savior's Infant Cries Were Heard   1

FREEDOM

Eagles' Spiralings Comply   12

FUTURE

View the Present Through the Promise   17
We Travel Toward a Land Unknown   16
When There Is No Star to Guide You   22

GRIEF

How Long, O Lord, How Long?   7

GUIDANCE

We Travel Toward a Land Unknown   16
When There Is No Star to Guide You   22

IMAGES OF GOD

Source and Sovereign, Rock and Cloud   20

INCLUSIVENESS

Source and Sovereign, Rock and Cloud   20

INSTALLATION

Pastor, Lead Our Circle Dance   15

JOURNEY

We Travel Toward a Land Unknown   16
When There Is No Star to Guide You   22

Hymn number

JUBILEES

We Travel Toward a Land Unknown 16

JUSTICE

Ask, Seek, Knock 21
Glory to God Is the Song of the Stars 8
God Made from One Blood all the
  Families of Earth 19
Holy and Good Is the Gift of Desire 18
Lions and Oxen Will Feed in the Hay 25
The Least in God's Kingdom Is Greater
  than John 23

KNOWLEDGE AND FAITH

Praise the Source of Faith and Learning 4
When There Is No Star to Guide You 22

LENT

How Long, O Lord, How Long? 7
The Cross on the Hill Is the Measuring
  Rod 11

LORD'S PRAYER

Let all Who Pray the Prayer Christ
  Taught 13

MARRIAGE

We Need Each Other's Voice to Sing 5
When There Is No Star to Guide You 22

MUSIC

Glory to God Is the Song of the Stars 8
Make Your Prayer and Music One 9
We Need Each Other's Voice to Sing 5

OUR FATHER

Let all Who Pray the Prayer Christ
  Taught 13

Hymn number

PEACE

Fierce the Force that Curled Cain's Fist 24
God Made from One Blood all the
  Families of Earth 19
Holy and Good Is the Gift of Desire 18
Lions and Oxen Will Feed in the Hay 25

PENTECOST

Eagles' Spiralings Comply 12
Through Our Fragmentary Prayers 14
We Travel Toward a Land Unknown 16

PRAYER

Ask, Seek, Knock 21
Let all Who Pray the Prayer Christ
  Taught 13
Make Your Prayer and Music One 9
Through Our Fragmentary Prayers 14

PREACHING

The Rocks Would Shout if We Kept Still 10

PRIORITIES

The Least in God's Kingdom Is Greater
  than John 23

PROCLAMATION

The Rocks Would Shout if We Kept Still 10

RESPONSIBILITY

Eagles' Spiralings Comply 12
When There Is No Star to Guide You 22

RESURRECTION

Risen Christ, May Death be Swift 6

SCIENCE AND FAITH

Praise the Source of Faith and Learning 4
When There Is No Star to Guide You 22

Hymn number

SEARCHING FAITH

Ask, Seek, Knock   21
When There Is No Star to Guide You   22

SEXISM

God Made from One Blood all the
    Families of Earth   19
Holy and Good Is the Gift of Desire   18
Source and Sovereign, Rock and Cloud   20

SEXUAL ATTRACTION

Holy and Good Is the Gift of Desire   18

TERMINAL ILLNESS

Risen Christ, May Death be Swift   6

VALUES

The Least in God's Kingdom Is Greater
    than John   23

Hymn number

VIOLENCE

Fierce the Force that Curled Cain's
    Fist   24
Lions and Oxen Will Feed in the Hay   25
Our Savior's Infant Cries Were
    Heard   1

VOCATION

Ask, Seek, Knock   21
When There Is No Star to Guide
    You   22

WEDDING

We Need Each Other's Voice to Sing   5
When There Is No Star to Guide You   22

WORD OF GOD

The Rocks Would Shout if We Kept
    Still   10

Index of First Lines

Hymn number

Ask, Seek, Knock	21
Eagles' Spiralings Comply	12
Fierce the Force that Curled Cain's Fist	24
Glory to God Is the Song of the Stars	8
God Made From One Blood all the Families of Earth	19
Holy and Good Is the Gift of Desire	18
how Long, O Lord, How Long?	7
If all You Want, Lord, Is My Heart	2
Let all Who Pray the Prayer Christ Taught	13
Lions and Oxen Will Feed in the Hay	25
Make Your Prayer and Music One	9
Our Savior's Infant Cries Were Heard	1
Pastor, Lead Our Circle Dance	15

Hymn number

Praise the Source of Faith and Learning	4
Risen Christ, May Death be Swift	6
Source and Sovereign, Rock and Cloud	20
The Cross on the Hill Is the Measuring Rod	11
The Least in God's Kingdom Is Greater than John	23
The Rocks Would Shout if We Kept Still	10
hrough Our Fragmentary Prayers	14
View the Present Through the Promise	17
We Need Each Other's Voice to Sing	5
We Travel Toward a Land Unknown	16
What King Would Wade Through Murky Streams	3
When There Is No Star to Guide You	22

Index of Alternate Tunes

The alternate tunes listed here are well-known traditional settings found in nearly any standard hymnal.

Hymn	Alternate tune
If all You Want, Lord, Is My Heart	St. Flavian
Let all Who Pray the Prayer Christ Taught	Crimond
Source and Sovereign, Rock and Cloud	St. George's Windsor
Fierce the Force that Curled Cain's Fist	Aberystwyth
Praise the Source of Faith and Learning	Hyfrydol

Hyms not included in this list feature unusual meters or have no suitable match to a well-known tune.